CW00693765

# BAKER STREET TO UXBRIDGE AND STANMORE

**Vic Mitchell and Keith Smith**

MP Middleton Press

*Cover picture: The "Camel-Back" electric locomotives were initially employed by the Metropolitan Railway to haul their long distance trains out as far as Harrow-on-the-Hill, usually. This train includes one of the line's two Pullman cars and it is about to be overtaken by a northbound Great Central express. (P.Q.Treloar coll.)*

*Published November 2006*

*ISBN     1 904474 90 X*
*978 1 904474 90 6*

*© Middleton Press, 2006*

*Design Deborah Esher*
*Typesetting Barbara Mitchell*

*Published by*
*Middleton Press*
*Easebourne Lane*
*Midhurst*
*West Sussex*
*GU29 9AZ*
*Tel: 01730 813169*
*Fax: 01730 812601*
*Email: info@middletonpress.co.uk*
*www.middletonpress.co.uk*

*Printed & bound by Biddles Ltd, Kings Lynn*

# INDEX

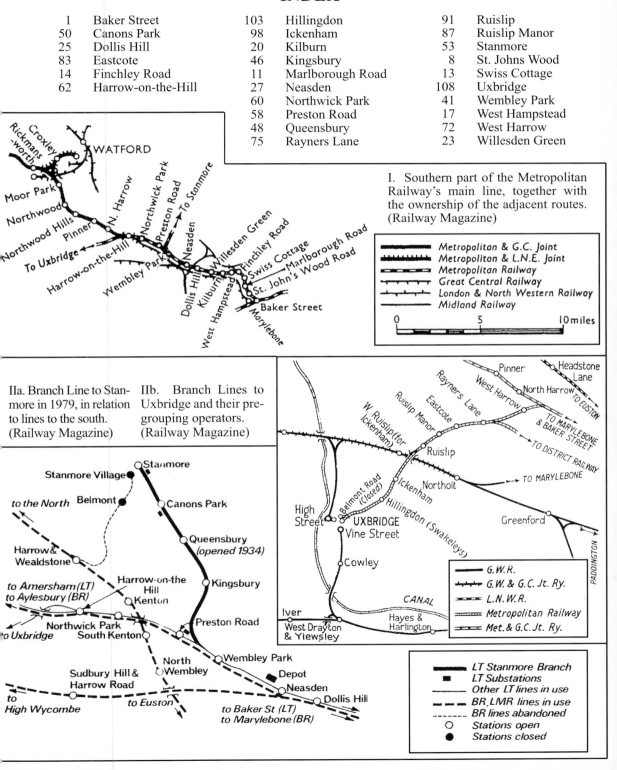

I. Southern part of the Metropolitan Railway's main line, together with the ownership of the adjacent routes. (Railway Magazine)

Metropolitan & G.C. Joint
Metropolitan & L.N.E. Joint
Metropolitan Railway
Great Central Railway
London & North Western Railway
Midland Railway

0      5      10miles

IIa. Branch Line to Stanmore in 1979, in relation to lines to the south. (Railway Magazine)

IIb. Branch Lines to Uxbridge and their pre-grouping operators. (Railway Magazine)

G.W.R.
G.W. & G.C. Jt. Ry.
L.N.W.R.
Metropolitan Railway
Met. & G.C. Jt. Ry.

LT Stanmore Branch
LT Substations
Other LT lines in use
BR,LMR lines in use
BR lines abandoned
Stations open
Stations closed

# ACKNOWLEDGEMENTS

We are grateful for the assistance received from many of those mentioned in the credits also to R.S.Carpenter, P.Chancellor, J.E.Connor, G.Croughton, Dr R.J.Harley, N.Langridge, J.H.Meredith, Mr D. and Dr S.Salter, R.Thompson (Harrow Local History Collection - HLHC), D.Wilson and particularly our wives, Barbara Mitchell and Janet Smith.

# GEOGRAPHICAL SETTING

Much of the first two miles of the route tunnels under the high ground forming the southern part of Hampstead Heath. After three miles of climbing the line descends to Neasden to cross the Brent Valley and then climbs to reach the elevated residential area of Harrow.

The Stanmore branch climbs through a series of cuttings to reach its terminus, which was originally in open country. It is about 300ft above sea level.

The Uxbridge line finishes at a lower level than its junction at Harrow, at a site close to the old town centre. This market town developed in the valley of the River Colne and was of such importance that it was served by two earlier branch lines, plus the Grand Union Canal.

The maps are to the scale of 25ins to 1 mile, with north at the top unless otherwise indicated.

# HISTORICAL BACKGROUND

Eventually to form part of the Circle Line, the Metropolitan Railway's route between Farringdon Street and Paddington opened in 1863. The Metropolitan & St. Johns Wood Railway branched north from it at Baker Street and came into use on 13th April 1868, to Swiss Cottage. The line was extended thus: to West Hampstead on 30th June 1879, to Willesden Green on 24th November 1879, to Harrow-on-the-Hill on 2nd August 1880 and to Pinner on 25th May 1885, Aylesbury eventually being reached in 1892. The Met had absorbed the M&SWR in 1882, having operated its services from the outset.

Meanwhile the Manchester, Sheffield & Lincolnshire Railway had expansionist plans aimed on London and its name was changed to the Great Central Railway in 1897. It made an agreement with the Met to operate over its route south of Quainton Road (which is north of Aylesbury) to a new terminus at Marylebone, this coming into use on 15th March 1899. North of Harrow, the line was jointly operated by the

Metropolitan & Great Central Committee after its formation in 1906. Each railway undertook most maintenance for alternate periods of five years. South of Harrow South Junction, the tracks continued to be owned by the Met, but the GCR obtained a long lease on the western pair.

The plan proved unsatisfactory for the GCR and it made alternative arrangements in Buckinghamshire, by using part of the Great Western Railway's direct route between London and Birmingham. The GCR built a line from Neasden westwards to Northolt to reach the GCR/GWR joint line, which opened on 2nd April 1906.

The Met started an electrification programme in 1904 on its underground lines, extending to Harrow and its new line from there to Uxbridge, which opened on 4th July of that year. This was electrically operated from 1st January 1905. The Rayners Lane-Uxbridge section received District Line trains from 1st March 1910 and these were replaced by Piccadilly Line trains from 23rd October

1933. The Met opened the Stanmore branch on 10th December 1932, using full size electric stock. Tube trains have operated it since 20th November 1939, when such tunnels were completed between Baker Street and Finchley Road. This service was part of the Bakerloo Line, the southern terminus of which had been Elephant & Castle since 1906. The branch became the northern part of the Jubilee Line on 1st May 1979, the other extremity of which was eventually to be at Stratford. New tunnels were provided south from Baker Street to Charing Cross from that date.

The Met came under the London Passenger Transport Board (LT) in 1933, the GCR having become a constituent of the London & North Eastern Railway (LNER) in 1923. Upon nationalisation in 1948, the LNER became largely the Eastern Region of British Railways, but the former LNER-operated services within this volume were transferred to the London Midland Region on 1st February 1958 and then to the Western Region on 11th October 1987. They became part of the Thames & Chiltern area of Network SouthEast at that time. With the advent of privatisation, a franchise was let on 21st July 1996 to M40 Trains for Chiltern Railways to operate all services from Marylebone for seven years. Owing to its success, an extension to 2021 followed.

# PASSENGER SERVICES

The April 1880 timetable showed trains at 10 minute intervals to Kilburn & Brondesbury and every 30 minutes to Willesden Green, with fewer on Sundays. The same frequency applied upon extension to Harrow-on-the-Hill in August 1880, Pinner in 1885 and Rickmansworth in 1887. Following the extension of services to Aylesbury in 1892, the 30 minute interval was cut back to Harrow, with trains approximately hourly north thereof except at peak times. They were still irregular by 1898, particularly on Sundays.

There were few changes to Met services with the advent of GCR trains in 1899. The first timetable to Uxbridge in 1904 showed one train in most hours, but three at peak times. By 1933, the off-peak service was given as "about every 30 minutes".

The initial Stanmore frequency was every 20 minutes off peak, with 7 trains per hour at busy times. Steady improvements after World War II led to the high frequency service which is offered today, on both routes. The Rayners Lane-Uxbridge section had been enhanced with the addition of District Line trains from 1st March 1910, these being replaced by those of the Piccadilly Line from 23rd October 1933.

Increased frequencies at the London end are provided by the use of reversal sidings at West Hampstead, Willesden Green, Wembley Park, Harrow-on-the-Hill and Rayners Lane.

October 1905

P.M. times are in heavy figures

## Metropolitan Line Uxbridge - Harrow - Wembley Park - Baker Street — 2

MONDAY to FRIDAY–morning

| No. 1. | | | | | J | | | | J | | | | K | | | | | | | | | | |
|---|---|---|---|---|---|---|---|---|---|---|---|---|---|---|---|---|---|---|---|---|---|---|---|
| UXBRIDGE | .... | .... | .... | .... | 455 | .... | 512 | .... | 527 | 541 | 556 | .... | 612 | 624 | .... | 636 | 646 | 653 | .... | 659 | 7 6 | 712 | .... |
| Hillingdon | .. | .. | .. | .. | 457 | .. | 514 | .. | 529 | 543 | 558 | .. | 614 | 626 | .. | 638 | 648 | 655 | .. | 7 1 | 7 8 | 714 | .. |
| Ickenham | .... | .... | .... | .... | 459 | .... | 516 | .... | 531 | 545 | 6 0 | .... | 616 | 628 | .... | 640 | 650 | 657 | .... | 7 3 | 710 | 716 | .... |
| Ruislip | .. | .. | .. | .. | 5 2 | .. | 519 | .. | 534 | 548 | 6 3 | .. | 619 | 631 | .. | 643 | 653 | 7 0 | .. | 7 6 | 713 | 719 | .. |
| Ruislip Manor | .... | .... | .... | .... | 5 3 | .... | 520 | .... | 535 | 549 | 6 4 | .... | 620 | 632 | .... | 644 | 654 | 7 1 | .... | 7 7 | 714 | 720 | .... |
| Eastcote | .. | .. | .. | .. | 5 5 | .. | 522 | .. | 537 | 551 | 6 6 | .. | 622 | 634 | .. | 646 | 656 | 7 3 | .. | 7 9 | 716 | 722 | .. |
| Rayners Lane | .... | .... | .... | .... | 510 | .... | 527 | .... | 542 | 556 | 611 | .... | 627 | 639 | .... | 651 | 7 1 | 7 8 | .... | 714 | 721 | 727 | .... |
| West Harrow | .. | .. | .. | .. | 512 | .. | 529 | .. | 544 | 558 | 613 | .. | 629 | 641 | .. | 653 | 7 3 | 710 | .. | 716 | 723 | 729 | .. |
| Harrow on the Hill | .... | 457 | .... | .... | 515 | 524 | 532 | 540 | 547 | 6 1 | 616 | 622 | 632 | 644 | 653 | 656 | 7 6 | 713 | 716 | 719 | 726 | 732 | 736 |
| Northwick Park | .. | 459 | .. | .. | 517 | 526 | 534 | 542 | 549 | 6 3 | 618 | 624 | 634 | 646 | 655 | 658 | 7 8 | 715 | 718 | 721 | 728 | 734 | 738 |
| Preston Road | H | 5 2 | H | .... | 520 | 529 | 537 | 545 | 552 | 6 6 | 621 | 627 | 637 | 649 | 658 | 7 1 | 711 | 718 | 721 | 724 | 731 | 737 | 741 |
| Wembley Park | 454 | 5 5 | 5 5 | .. | 522 | 531 | 539 | 547 | 554 | 610 | 624 | 629 | 639 | 651 | 7 0 | 7 4 | 713 | 721 | 724 | 727 | 733 | 739 | 744 |
| Finchley Road | 5 7 | 513 | 518 | .... | 532 | 539 | 548 | 555 | 6 4 | 618 | 632 | 637 | 649 | 659 | 7 9 | 713 | 721 | 729 | 732 | 735 | 741 | 747 | 752 |
| BAKER STREET | 512 | 518 | 523 | .. | 537 | 544 | 553 | 6 0 | 6 9 | 623 | 637 | 642 | 654 | 7 4 | 714 | 718 | 726 | 734 | 737 | 740 | 746 | 752 | 757 |
| Kings Cross St. Pancras | 519 | .... | .... | .... | .... | .... | .... | .... | .... | .... | .... | .... | .... | .... | .... | 725 | .... | .... | 745 | 748 | .... | .... | 8 6 |
| Moorgate | 525 | .. | .. | .. | .. | .. | .. | .. | .. | .. | .. | .. | .. | .. | .. | 731 | .. | .. | 751 | 754 | .. | .. | 812 |
| Liverpool Street | 527 | .... | .... | .... | .... | .... | .... | .... | .... | .... | .... | .... | .... | .... | .... | 733 | .... | .... | .... | 756 | .... | .... | 814 |
| ALDGATE | .. | .. | .. | .. | .. | .. | .. | .. | .. | .. | .. | .. | .. | .. | .. | 735 | .. | .. | .. | 758 | .. | .. | 816 |

P.M. times are in heavy figures

## Metropolitan Line Uxbridge - Harrow - Wembley Park - Baker Street — 2

MONDAY to FRIDAY–morning

| No. 2. | | | | | | | | | | | | | | | | | | | | | | | |
|---|---|---|---|---|---|---|---|---|---|---|---|---|---|---|---|---|---|---|---|---|---|---|---|
| UXBRIDGE | 719 | 727 | .... | 735 | .... | 743 | 750 | 756 | .... | 8 2 | .... | 8 8 | .... | 815 | .... | 821 | 827 | .... | 833 | 840 | .... | 847 | .... |
| Hillingdon | 721 | 729 | .. | 737 | .. | 745 | 752 | 758 | .. | 8 4 | .. | 810 | .. | 817 | .. | 823 | 829 | .. | 835 | 842 | .. | 849 | .. |
| Ickenham | 723 | 731 | .... | 739 | .... | 747 | 754 | 8 0 | .... | 8 6 | .... | 812 | .... | 819 | .... | 825 | 831 | .... | 837 | 844 | .... | 851 | .... |
| Ruislip | 726 | 734 | .. | 742 | .. | 750 | 757 | 8 3 | .. | 8 9 | .. | 815 | .. | 822 | .. | 828 | 834 | .. | 840 | 847 | .. | 854 | .. |
| Ruislip Manor | 727 | 735 | .... | 743 | .... | 751 | 758 | 8 4 | .... | 810 | .... | 816 | .... | 823 | .... | 829 | 835 | .... | 841 | 848 | .... | 855 | .... |
| Eastcote | 729 | 737 | .. | 745 | .. | 753 | 8 0 | 8 6 | .. | 812 | .. | 818 | .. | 825 | .. | 831 | 837 | .. | 843 | 850 | .. | 857 | .. |
| Rayners Lane | 734 | 742 | .... | 750 | .... | 758 | 8 5 | 811 | .... | 817 | .... | 823 | .... | 830 | .... | 836 | 842 | .... | 848 | 854 | .... | 9 1 | .... |
| West Harrow | 736 | 744 | .. | 752 | .. | 8 1 | 8 7 | 813 | .. | 819 | .. | 825 | .. | 832 | .. | 839 | 845 | .. | 851 | 856 | .. | 9 3 | .. |
| Harrow on the Hill | 739 | 747 | 752 | 755 | 8 1 | 8 4 | 810 | 816 | 819 | 822 | 826 | 828 | 833 | 835 | 840 | 842 | 848 | 852 | 854 | 859 | 9 2 | 9 7 | 912 |
| Northwick Park | 741 | 749 | 754 | 757 | 8 3 | 8 6 | 812 | 818 | 821 | 824 | 828 | 830 | 835 | 837 | 842 | 844 | 850 | 854 | 856 | 9 1 | 9 4 | 9 9 | 914 |
| Preston Road | 744 | 752 | 757 | 8 0 | 8 6 | 8 9 | 815 | 822 | 824 | 827 | 831 | 833 | 838 | 840 | 845 | 847 | 854 | 857 | 859 | 9 4 | 9 7 | 913 | 917 |
| Wembley Park | 746 | 754 | 759 | 8 2 | 8 8 | 811 | 817 | 824 | 827 | 829 | 834 | 836 | 841 | 843 | 848 | 850 | 857 | 859 | 9 2 | 9 7 | 9 9 | 916 | 919 |
| Finchley Road | 754 | 8 2 | 8 7 | 810 | 817 | 819 | 826 | 833 | 835 | 838 | 842 | 844 | 849 | 851 | 856 | 858 | 9 5 | 9 8 | 910 | 915 | 918 | 925 | 928 |
| BAKER STREET | 759 | 8 7 | 813 | 815 | 822 | 824 | 831 | 838 | 840 | 843 | 847 | 849 | 854 | 856 | 9 1 | 9 3 | 911 | 913 | 916 | 920 | 923 | 930 | 933 |
| Kings Cross St. Pancras | .... | 814 | 821 | .... | .... | 832 | 840 | .... | 847 | 851 | 855 | .... | .... | 9 3 | .... | 910 | .... | 921 | .... | 928 | .... | .... | 940 |
| Moorgate | .. | 820 | 827 | .. | .. | 838 | 846 | .. | 853 | 857 | 9 1 | .. | .. | 9 9 | .. | 916 | .. | 927 | .. | 934 | .. | .. | 946 |
| Liverpool Street | .... | 822 | 829 | .... | .... | 840 | 848 | .... | 855 | 859 | 9 3 | .... | .... | 911 | .... | .... | .... | 929 | .... | 936 | .... | .... | 948 |
| ALDGATE | .. | 824 | 831 | .. | .. | 842 | 850 | .. | 857 | 9 1 | 9 5 | .. | .. | 913 | .. | .. | .. | 931 | .. | 938 | .. | .. | 950 |

MONDAY to FRIDAY–morning

| No. 3. | | | | | | | | | | | | | | | | | | | | | | |
|---|---|---|---|---|---|---|---|---|---|---|---|---|---|---|---|---|---|---|---|---|---|---|
| UXBRIDGE | 856 | 9 6 | .... | .... | 919 | 933 | 946 | 10 0 | | 13 | 28 | 43 | 58 | | 213 | 228 | .... | 243 | 258 | 313 | 328 | 343 |
| Hillingdon | 858 | 9 8 | .. | .. | 921 | 935 | 948 | 10 2 | | 15 | 30 | 45 | 0 | | 215 | 230 | .. | 245 | 3 0 | 315 | 330 | 345 |
| Ickenham | 9 0 | 910 | .... | .... | 923 | 937 | 950 | 10 4 | | 17 | 32 | 47 | 2 | | 217 | 232 | .... | 247 | 3 2 | 317 | 332 | 347 |
| Ruislip | 9 3 | 913 | .. | .. | 926 | 940 | 953 | 10 7 | | 20 | 35 | 50 | 5 | | 220 | 235 | .. | 250 | 3 5 | 320 | 335 | 350 |
| Ruislip Manor | 9 4 | 914 | .... | .... | 927 | 941 | 954 | 10 8 | Then | 21 | 36 | 51 | 6 | | 221 | 236 | .... | 251 | 3 6 | 321 | 336 | 351 |
| Eastcote | 9 6 | 916 | .. | .. | 929 | 943 | 956 | 1010 | at | 23 | 38 | 53 | 8 | | 223 | 238 | .. | 253 | 3 8 | 323 | 338 | 353 |
| Rayners Lane | 910 | 920 | .... | .... | 933 | 947 | 10 0 | 1014 | these | 27 | 42 | 57 | 12 | | 227 | 242 | .... | 257 | 312 | 327 | 342 | 357 |
| West Harrow | 912 | 922 | .. | .. | 935 | 949 | 10 2 | 1016 | minutes | 29 | 44 | 59 | 14 | UNTIL | 229 | 244 | .. | 259 | 314 | 329 | 344 | 359 |
| Harrow on the Hill | 916 | 925 | 928 | 936 | 940 | 953 | 10 6 | 1020 | past | 32 | 47 | 2 | 17 | | 232 | 247 | .... | 3 2 | 317 | 332 | 347 | 4 2 |
| Northwick Park | 918 | 927 | 930 | 938 | 942 | 955 | 10 8 | 1022 | each | 34 | 49 | 4 | 19 | | 234 | 249 | .. | 3 4 | 319 | 334 | 349 | 4 4 |
| Preston Road | 922 | 930 | 933 | 941 | 945 | 958 | 1011 | 1025 | hour | 37 | 52 | 7 | 22 | | 237 | 252 | .... | 3 7 | 322 | 337 | 352 | 4 7 |
| Wembley Park | 924 | 932 | 935 | 943 | 947 | 10 0 | 1013 | 1027 | | 40 | 55 | 10 | 25 | | 240 | 254 | .. | 310 | 324 | 341 | 355 | 410 |
| Finchley Road | 933 | 940 | 944 | 951 | 955 | 10 8 | 1021 | 1035 | | 48 | 3 | 18 | 33 | | 248 | 3 3 | .... | 318 | 332 | 349 | 4 3 | 418 |
| BAKER STREET | 938 | 945 | 949 | 956 | 10 0 | 1013 | 1026 | 1040 | | 53 | 8 | 23 | 38 | | 253 | 3 8 | .. | 323 | 337 | 354 | 4 8 | 423 |
| Kings Cross St. Pancras | .... | 952 | 956 | .... | 10 7 | .... | .... | .... | | .... | .... | .... | .... | | .... | .... | .... | 332 | .... | 4 2 | 417 | .... |
| Moorgate | .. | 958 | 10 2 | .. | 1013 | .. | .. | .. | | .. | .. | .. | .. | | .. | .. | .. | 338 | .. | 4 8 | 423 | .. |
| Liverpool Street | .... | 10 0 | 10 4 | .... | 1015 | .... | .... | .... | | .... | .... | .... | .... | | .... | .... | .... | 340 | .... | 410 | 425 | .... |
| ALDGATE | .. | 10 2 | 10 6 | .. | 1017 | .. | .. | .. | | .. | .. | .. | .. | | .. | .. | .. | 342 | .. | 412 | 427 | .. |

P.M. times are in heavy figures

## Metropolitan Line Uxbridge - Harrow - Wembley Park - Baker Street — 2

MONDAY to FRIDAY–afternoon

| No. 4. | | | | | | | | | | | | | | | | | | | | | | | | | | | |
|---|---|---|---|---|---|---|---|---|---|---|---|---|---|---|---|---|---|---|---|---|---|---|---|---|---|---|---|
| UXBRIDGE | 358 | .... | 413 | 428 | .... | 443 | .... | 458 | .... | 5 8 | .... | 518 | .... | 528 | .... | 537 | .... | 548 | .... | 558 | 6 8 | .... | 619 | .... | 631 | .... | 643 |
| Hillingdon | 4 0 | .. | 415 | 430 | .. | 445 | .. | 5 0 | .. | 510 | .. | 520 | .. | 530 | .. | 539 | .. | 550 | .. | 6 0 | 610 | .. | 621 | .. | 633 | .. | 645 |
| Ickenham | 4 2 | .... | 417 | 432 | .... | 447 | .... | 5 2 | .... | 512 | .... | 522 | .... | 532 | .... | 541 | .... | 552 | .... | 6 2 | 612 | .... | 623 | .... | 635 | .... | 647 |
| Ruislip | 4 5 | .. | 420 | 435 | .. | 450 | .. | 5 5 | .. | 515 | .. | 525 | .. | 535 | .. | 543 | .. | 555 | .. | 6 5 | 615 | .. | 626 | .. | 638 | .. | 650 |
| Ruislip Manor | 4 6 | .... | 421 | 436 | .... | 451 | .... | 5 6 | .... | 516 | .... | 526 | .... | 536 | .... | 544 | .... | 556 | .... | 6 6 | 616 | .... | 627 | .... | 639 | .... | 651 |
| Eastcote | 4 8 | .. | 423 | 438 | .. | 453 | .. | 5 8 | .. | 518 | .. | 528 | .. | 538 | .. | 546 | .. | 558 | .. | 6 8 | 618 | .. | 629 | .. | 641 | .. | 653 |
| Rayners Lane | 412 | .... | 427 | 442 | .... | 457 | .... | 512 | .... | 522 | .... | 532 | .... | 542 | .... | 551 | .... | 6 2 | .... | 613 | 623 | .... | 633 | .... | 645 | .... | 657 |
| West Harrow | 414 | .. | 429 | 444 | .. | 459 | .. | 514 | .. | 524 | .. | 534 | .. | 544 | .. | 553 | .. | 6 4 | .. | 615 | 625 | .. | 635 | .. | 647 | .. | 659 |
| Harrow on the Hill | 417 | 427 | 433 | 447 | 458 | 5 3 | 511 | 517 | 521 | 527 | 534 | 537 | 545 | 547 | 554 | 556 | 6 3 | 6 7 | 616 | 618 | 628 | 635 | 638 | 647 | 650 | 657 | 7 3 |
| Northwick Park | 419 | 429 | 435 | 449 | 5 0 | 5 5 | 513 | 519 | \| | 529 | 536 | 539 | \| | 549 | \| | 558 | 6 5 | 6 9 | \| | 620 | 630 | 637 | 640 | 649 | 652 | 659 | 7 5 |
| Preston Road | 422 | 432 | 438 | 452 | 5 3 | 5 8 | 516 | 522 | \| | 532 | 539 | 542 | \| | 552 | \| | 6 1 | 6 8 | 612 | \| | 623 | 633 | 640 | 643 | 652 | 655 | 7 2 | 7 8 |
| Wembley Park | 425 | 434 | 440 | 454 | 5 5 | 510 | 518 | 524 | 527 | 534 | 541 | 544 | 552 | 554 | 6 0 | 6 4 | 611 | 614 | 622 | 626 | 635 | 642 | 645 | 654 | 657 | 7 4 | 710 |
| Finchley Road | 433 | 442 | 448 | 5 2 | 514 | 519 | 527 | 533 | 536 | 543 | 549 | 552 | 6 0 | 6 3 | 6 9 | 613 | 619 | B6 25 | 631 | B6 36 | B6 46 | 650 | B6 56 | 7 2 | B7 8 | 713 | 7 8 |
| BAKER STREET | 438 | 447 | 453 | 5 7 | 519 | 524 | 532 | 538 | 541 | 548 | 554 | 558 | 6 5 | 6 8 | 614 | 618 | 624 | B6 31 | 636 | B6 41 | B6 51 | 655 | B7 1 | 7 7 | B7 13 | 719 | 723 |
| Kings Cross St. Pancras | .... | 455 | 5 2 | .... | .... | 532 | 540 | .... | 547 | 555 | 6 3 | .... | .... | 615 | 625 | .... | .... | .... | .... | .... | .... | .... | .... | .... | .... | .... | .... |
| Moorgate | .. | 5 1 | 5 8 | .. | .. | 538 | 546 | .. | 553 | 6 1 | 6 9 | .. | .. | 621 | 631 | .. | .. | .. | .. | .. | .. | .. | .. | .. | .. | .. | .. |
| Liverpool Street | .... | 5 3 | 510 | .... | .... | 540 | 548 | .... | 555 | 6 3 | 611 | .... | .... | .... | 633 | .... | .... | .... | .... | .... | .... | .... | .... | .... | .... | .... | .... |
| ALDGATE | .. | 5 5 | 512 | .. | .. | 542 | 550 | .. | 557 | 6 5 | 613 | .. | .. | .. | 635 | .. | .. | .. | .. | .. | .. | .. | .. | .. | .. | .. | .. |

MONDAY to FRIDAY–night

| No. 5. | H | | | | | | | | | | | | | | | | | | | | H | H | |
|---|---|---|---|---|---|---|---|---|---|---|---|---|---|---|---|---|---|---|---|---|---|---|---|
| UXBRIDGE | 655 | .... | 710 | 725 | 740 | 755 | 810 | 825 | 840 | 855 | 910 | 925 | 940 | 955 | 1010 | 1025 | 1040 | 1055 | 1110 | 1126 | 1143 | 12 1 | 1230 |
| Hillingdon | 657 | .. | 712 | 727 | 742 | 757 | 812 | 827 | 842 | 857 | 912 | 927 | 942 | 957 | 1012 | 1027 | 1042 | 1057 | 1112 | 1128 | 1145 | 12 3 | 1232 |
| Ickenham | 659 | .... | 714 | 729 | 744 | 759 | 814 | 829 | 844 | 859 | 914 | 929 | 944 | 959 | 1014 | 1029 | 1044 | 1059 | 1114 | 1130 | 1147 | 12 5 | 1235 |
| Ruislip | 7 2 | .. | 717 | 732 | 747 | 8 2 | 817 | 832 | 847 | 9 2 | 917 | 932 | 947 | 10 2 | 1017 | 1032 | 1047 | 11 2 | 1117 | 1133 | 1150 | 12 8 | 1237 |
| Ruislip Manor | 7 3 | .... | 718 | 733 | 748 | 8 3 | 818 | 833 | 848 | 9 3 | 918 | 933 | 948 | 10 3 | 1018 | 1033 | 1048 | 11 3 | 1118 | 1134 | 1151 | 12 9 | 1238 |
| Eastcote | 7 5 | .. | 720 | 735 | 750 | 8 5 | 820 | 835 | 850 | 9 5 | 920 | 935 | 950 | 10 5 | 1020 | 1035 | 1050 | 11 5 | 1120 | 1136 | 1153 | 1211 | 1240 |
| Rayners Lane | 7 9 | .... | 724 | 739 | 754 | 8 9 | 824 | 839 | 854 | 9 9 | 924 | 939 | 954 | 10 9 | 1024 | 1039 | 1054 | 11 9 | 1124 | 1140 | 1157 | 1215 | 1244 |
| West Harrow | 711 | .. | 726 | 741 | 756 | 811 | 826 | 841 | 856 | 911 | 926 | 941 | 956 | 1011 | 1026 | 1041 | 1056 | 1111 | 1126 | 1142 | 1159 | 1217 | 1246 |
| Harrow on the Hill | 714 | 720 | 729 | 744 | 759 | 814 | 829 | 844 | 859 | 914 | 930 | 944 | 959 | 1014 | 1030 | 1044 | 11 0 | 1114 | 1129 | 1146 | 12 2 | 1220 | 1249 |
| Northwick Park | 716 | 722 | 731 | 746 | 8 1 | 816 | 831 | 846 | 9 1 | 916 | 932 | 946 | 10 1 | 1016 | 1032 | 1046 | 11 2 | 1116 | 1131 | 1148 | 12 4 | 1222 | 1251 |
| Preston Road | 719 | 725 | 734 | 749 | 8 4 | 819 | 834 | 849 | 9 4 | 919 | 935 | 949 | 10 4 | 1019 | 1035 | 1049 | 11 5 | 1119 | 1134 | 1151 | 12 7 | 1225 | 1254 |
| Wembley Park | 721 | 727 | 736 | 751 | 8 6 | 821 | 837 | 851 | 9 6 | 923 | 937 | 953 | 10 7 | 1021 | 1037 | 1051 | 11 7 | 1121 | 1136 | 1154 | 1211 | 1227 | 1256 |
| Finchley Road | 729 | 735 | B7 47 | 759 | 814 | 829 | 845 | 9 0 | 915 | 931 | 946 | 10 2 | 1015 | 1029 | 1045 | 11 0 | 1116 | B11 34 | 1144 | 12 2 | 1223 | 1240 | .... |
| BAKER STREET | 734 | 740 | B7 52 | 8 4 | 819 | 834 | 850 | 9 5 | 920 | 936 | 951 | 10 7 | 1020 | 1034 | 1050 | 11 5 | 1121 | B11 39 | 1149 | 12 7 | 1228 | 1245 | .. |
| Kings Cross St. Pancras | .... | .... | .... | .... | .... | .... | .... | .... | .... | .... | .... | .... | .... | .... | .... | .... | .... | .... | .... | .... | .... | .... | .... |
| Moorgate | .. | .. | .. | .. | .. | .. | .. | .. | .. | .. | .. | .. | .. | .. | .. | .. | .. | .. | .. | .. | .. | .. | .. |
| Liverpool Street | .... | .... | .... | .... | .... | .... | .... | .... | .... | .... | .... | .... | .... | .... | .... | .... | .... | .... | .... | .... | .... | .... | .... |
| ALDGATE | .. | .. | .. | .. | .. | .. | .. | .. | .. | .. | .. | .. | .. | .. | .. | .. | .. | .. | .. | .. | .. | .. | .. |

# MARYLEBONE TO RICKMANSWORTH

*This is the title of a companion album in which we study in detail the almost parallel GCR route, giving less attention to the Met stations than herein. Students of the route to Harrow-on-the-Hill and of the exhibition site at Wembley Park are advised to consult this volume, published in February 2005. To update it regarding notable developments at Marylebone, we include two views from 11th August 2006.*

i.       *A panorama towards the buffers has the new platform 6 on the right, it having come into use on 8th May 2006. Two of the original roof spans remain on the left. Platform 4 was reduced in length at its southern end and rebuilt. In revised form, it came into use, along with the new No. 5, on 18th September 2006. (V.Mitchell)*

ii.      *Carriage sidings stood on the site previously, but the entire station had been threatened with closure in 1984. This northward view looks towards the emergency exit up to the road bridge. The replica canopy is authentic in every detail. (V.Mitchell)*

# BAKER STREET

1.      The station opened on 10th January 1863 and was served by trains running between Farringdon Street and Paddington initially. A major rebuilding plan began in 1911. Loco smoke would issue intermittently from gratings in traffic islands until electrification in 1904. (G.Kerley coll./HLHC)

2.      The first sub-surface ticket hall came into use in about 1911 and was photographed around 20 years later. Broad gauge trains from the GWR could use the route until 1869 and meat trains to Smithfield Market passed through for almost another 100 years. (G.Kerley coll./HLHC)

3.	The largest part of the rebuild took place in 1927-30 when Chiltern Court was erected over the station, the main entrance to which is under the roof on the right of this view from about 1930. The way into the 1923 ticket hall is to the right of the bus. (G.Kerley coll./HLHC)

4.	A single line branch platform came into use in 1868, but it seems that there was little through running until 1907, owing to a movable platform having to be repositioned each time. Additional platforms came into use in the early 1890s, but they formed a separate station until 1898. The arrangement since is seen here in 1957, it comprising two central through lines and two bays. This is an example of T stock. (N.Simmons)

5.    A 1961 view features the eastern siding for the layover of locomotives and also an inspection pit, a legacy of steam days. Many loco-hauled trains continued to Liverpool Street. (J.C.Gillham)

III.  Contemporary track diagram, with the Circle Line on the right.

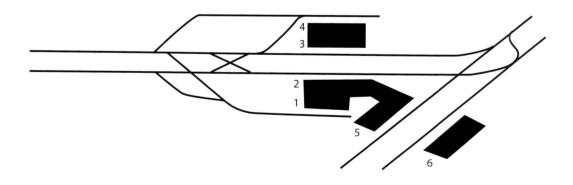

6.     The western siding was still used in 1961 for wagons of coal for the boilers of Chiltern House. After the siding was lifted, the platform was straightened. LOO LINE refers to the Bakerloo. With the advent of the Jubilee service in 1979, Baker Street had ten platforms. (J.C.Gillham)

7.     Seen on the outer lines in August 2006 are terminating trains, the other being an Amersham-Aldgate service. The double track connection to the Circle Line was brought into use on 4th November 1912, it then being known as the Inner Circle. (V.Mitchell)

# ST. JOHNS WOOD

←———

8.    The name shown above the entrance was in use until 1st April 1925. The station opened on 13th April 1868 and Swiss Cottage was the terminus until 30th June 1879. (G.Kerley coll./HLHC)

←———

9.    The platforms were recorded in about 1934. The station was renamed "Lords" in June 1939 and closed on 20th November of that year, when a new "St. Johns Wood" opened on the Bakerloo Line. (G.Kerley/HLHC)

10.    The second building was photographed on 26th June 1947, in non-railway use. Its location is shown at the top of map IV in *Marylebone to Rickmansworth*. It was constructed in the early 1920s and its site is now obscured by the Westmoreland Hotel. (G.Kerley/HLHC)

# MARLBOROUGH ROAD

11.     Two undated views show the station, which opened with the line to Swiss Cottage in 1868. It was on the corner of Finchley Road and Queen's Grove and the building became an Angus Steak House in the 1970s. (G.Kerley/HLHC)

12.     Like its southern neighbour, this station closed with the extension of the Bakerloo Line on 20th November 1939. (G.Kerley/HLHC)

# SWISS COTTAGE

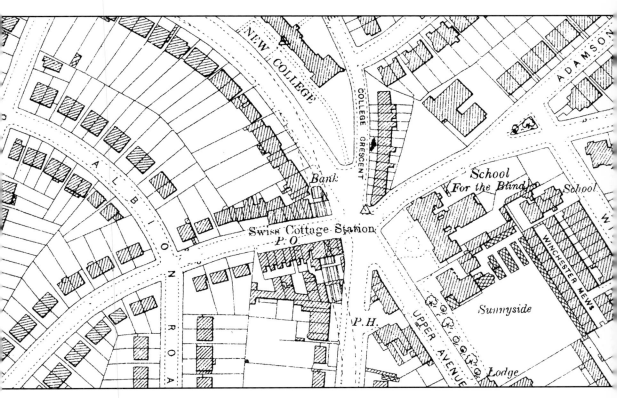

IV.    The 1894 survey indicates short sections of track open for ventilation.

13.    An Edwardian postcard reveals trades long forgotten and a station likewise. It was closed and replaced by one on the Bakerloo Line on 17th August 1940. It had been the terminus of the line until 30th June 1879 and still retained a trailing crossover in 1994. (P.M.Cowan coll.)

# FINCHLEY ROAD

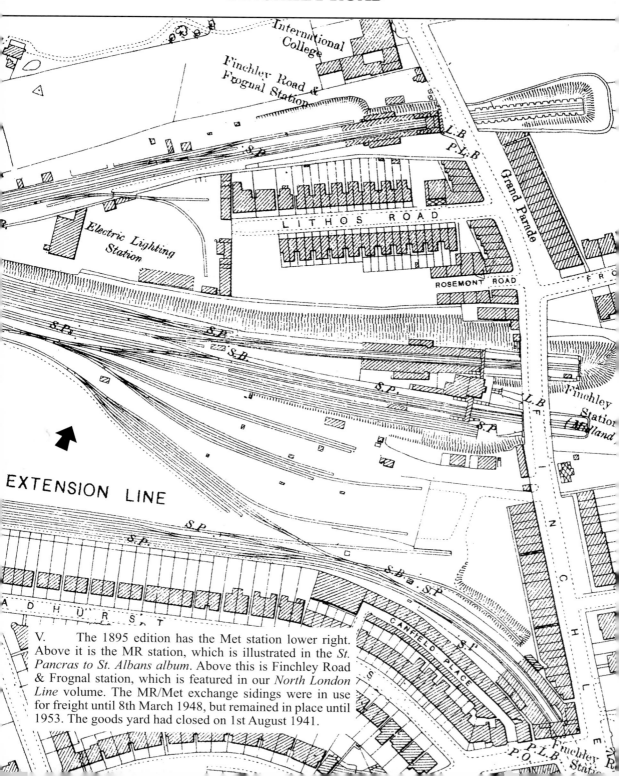

International College

Finchley Road & Frognal Station

Electric Lighting Station

L.B

P.L.B

LITHOS ROAD

ROSEMONT ROAD

Grand Parade

S.P.

S.P.

S.B.

S.P.

S.P.

L.B

Finchley Station (Midland)

S.P.

↖ EXTENSION LINE

S.P.

S.P.

S.B. a SP

A D H U R S T

CANFIELD PLACE

S.P.

Finchley Station

P.L.B

P.O.

V.    The 1895 edition has the Met station lower right.
Above it is the MR station, which is illustrated in the *St.
Pancras to St. Albans album*. Above this is Finchley Road
& Frognal station, which is featured in our *North London
Line* volume. The MR/Met exchange sidings were in use
for freight until 8th March 1948, but remained in place until
1953. The goods yard had closed on 1st August 1941.

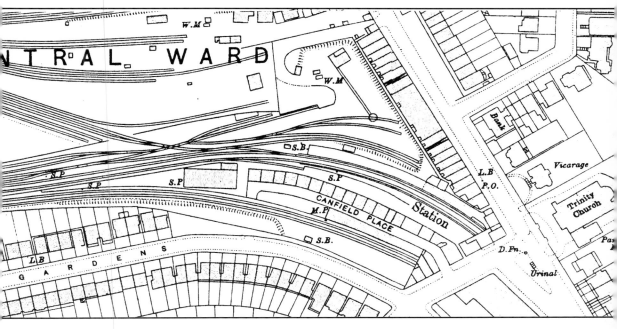

VI.    The 1915 map has the GCR tracks at the bottom. Comparison of the extracts will reveal the extent of the demolition that took place for their creation, notably on the south side of Canfield Place.

14.    Until major alterations in 1914, the ticket hall had natural lighting and its entrance on the south side. A two-storey stone-faced building was erected, with entrances in the south and east elevations. (G.Kerley coll./HLHC)

15.    The 1938 rebuild gave two central platforms for the Bakerloo line extension and two outer ones for Met trains. The first was completed many years before the northern one and is seen with Bo-Bo no. 10 *William Ewart Gladstone*. An overall roof was eventually completed. (Stations UK)

16.    The corner was cut off the building in 1938 and a single entrance was inserted in the new facade. The much altered structure was photographed in February 1987. The suffix "South Hampstead" was appended between about 1885 and 1914. (D.A.Thompson)

# WEST HAMPSTEAD

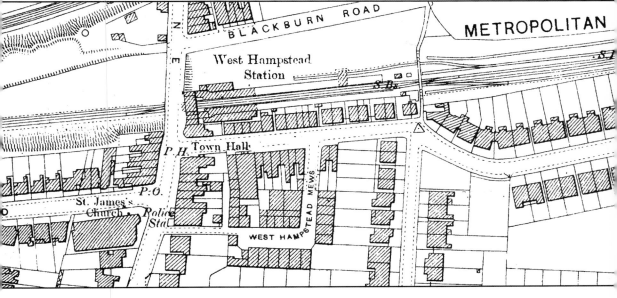

VII.    The 1895 survey shows two platforms and a goods shed. All vanished soon after.

17.    The island platform was photographed on 26th February 1938, shortly before it was demolished and rebuilt one track width to the right. Met quadrupling from Finchley Road to a site in the distance was completed on 30th November 1913. It was extended to Willesden Green on 31st May 1915. (G.Kerley/HLHC)

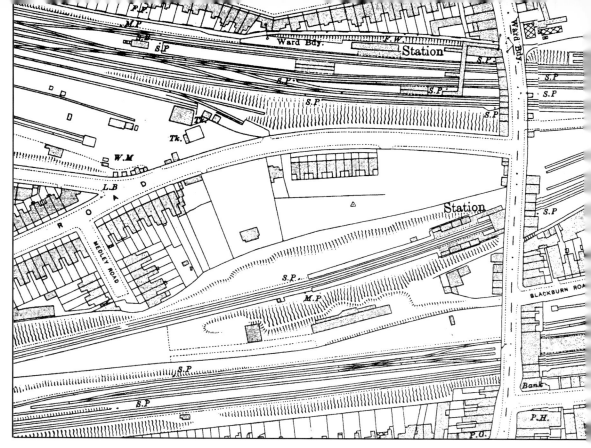

18.     The 1897 buildings were erected on a new road bridge and were photographed in about 1930. Their outline was little changed in 2006 and one reversal siding was still in use. (G.Kerley coll./HLHC)

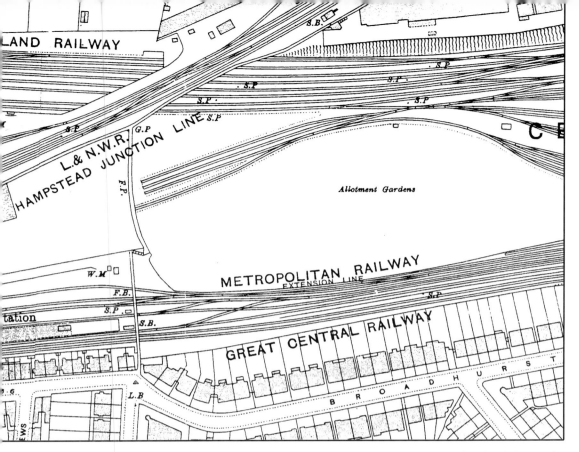

The following labels appear on the map:

LAND RAILWAY

S.B.

C E

L. & N.W.R.
HAMPSTEAD JUNCTION LINE  S.P
G.P

F.P.

*Allotment Gardens*

W.M

F.B.

S.P.

METROPOLITAN RAILWAY
EXTENSION LINE

S.P.

tation

S.B.

GREAT CENTRAL RAILWAY

B R O A D H U R S T

EWS

L.B

.6

VIII.   The station was completely reconstructed in 1897-98 to make space for the GCR tracks and a new island platform was built for Met trains, as shown on this 1915 map, which continues from no. VI. Note that there are reversing sidings west of the station.

19.   A westward view in 1959 makes worthwhile comparison with picture 17, as it shows the new position of the platform in relation to the building on the bridge and the spans below it. (Stations UK)

# KILBURN

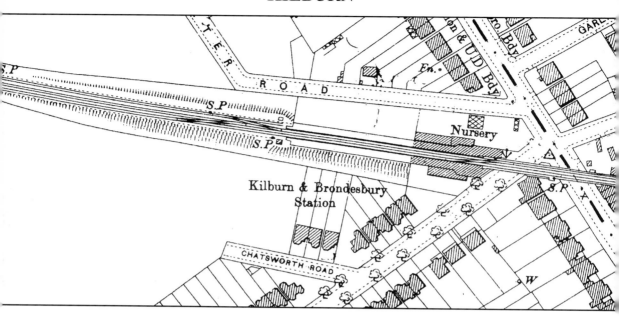

IX.    The 1893 survey has dots and dashes in Edgware Road, which was earlier the Roman Watling Street.

20.    The 1879 bridge is at the left border of this northward view from about 1934; it was replaced in 1977. The span on the right dates from 1914 and was still in use in 2006. The suffix AND BRONDESBURY was used until 25th September 1950. (G.Kerley coll./HLHC)

21.     A consistent style was presented in the 1930s, but subsequent alterations and additions have resulted in an unfortunate and unattractive mixture of features. (G.Kerley coll./HLHC)

22.     The platforms were recorded in April 1937, shortly before an island platform for tube trains replaced them. Bakerloo trains would use the centre two of the four LT tracks. (G.Kerley/HLHC)

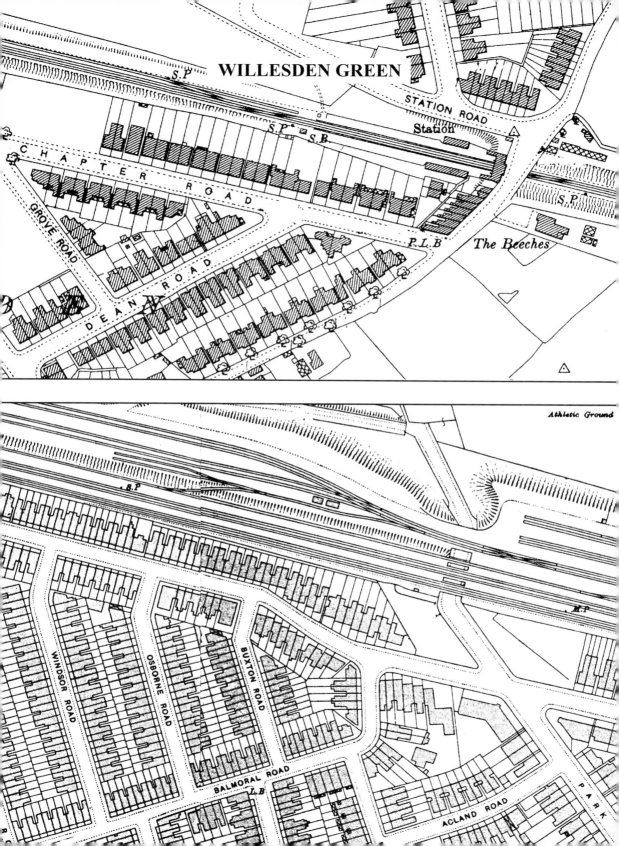

# WILLESDEN GREEN

*S.P*

STATION ROAD

*S.P.* *S.B*

Station

CHAPTER ROAD

GROVE ROAD

DEAN ROAD

*P.L.B*

The Beeches

*S.P.*

Athletic Ground

*.S.P*

*M.P*

WINDSOR ROAD

OSBORNE ROAD

BUXTON ROAD

BALMORAL ROAD

*L.B*

ACLAND ROAD

PARK

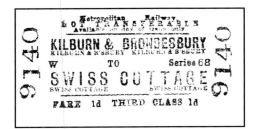

← X. The 1893 map includes undeveloped fields and a single goods siding.

XI.    Quadrupling from here to Neasden on 4th January 1914 was completed too late to be shown on this 1915 edition. (The lower two tracks are those of the GCR and date from 1899.) The reversing siding was moved to a central position between the four Met tracks. The goods yard opened on 13th October 1880 and received coal, building materials, fish, milk, fruit and other foods. Goods outward included machinery, snooker equipment, pencils and fireplaces. Traffic ceased on 3rd January 1966. Near the goods shed is a crane (Cr.), which was rated at 30cwt. Although LT handed over Met goods services to the LNER in November 1937, Willesden Green yard was an exception and remained under LT control until May 1962, when the LMR took over.

23.    The entrance building was completed in 1925 and photographed in 1930. There had previously been a small cottage-style structure at platform level. A bay platform was added in 1906, for use by terminating trains. The shape of the clock matched the platform nameboards of the period. (G.Kerley coll./HLHC)

24.    The suffix AND CRICKLEWOOD was in use from 1894 until 1938. Seen in 1960, the outer platforms were seldom used after 1940. The houses on the left were Met property. (Stations UK)

# DOLLIS HILL

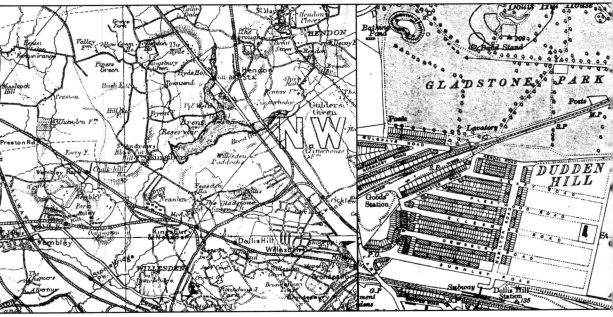

XII.    Bacon's 1 inch to 1 mile map of about 1910 (left) shows the rural location of the station, which opened on 1st October 1909. On the right is an extract from the 1920 edition at 6 ins to 1 mile, which indicates the proximity of Dollis Hill itself at 209ft above sea level.

25.    The GCR lines are on the right in this view towards London from April 1937. The platform was soon to be rebuilt to the left. The brackets at the guard's end of each platform carried two uninsulated wires which he connected with the brass handle of his flag to give a "Right Away" signal to the driver by means of a bell at the opposite end of the platform. (G.Kerley/HLHC)

26.　　The additional track on the right is evident in this 1960 photograph. The curved waiting room and roof design was employed at Kilburn in 1938, but here the ticket office is under the platform in an unattractive public subway. (Stations UK)

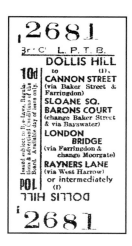

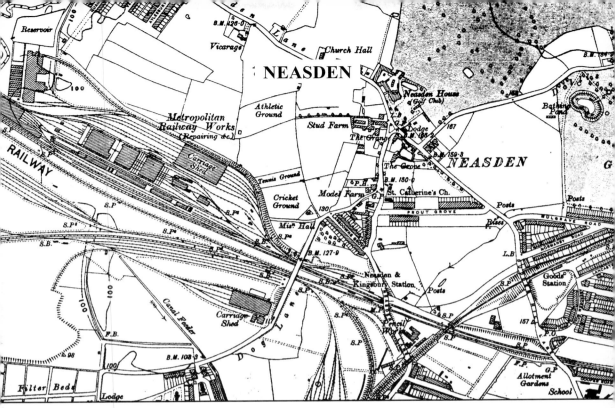

XIII.    Our route runs from right (lower) to left (upper); below the latter is the GCR line to the
GWR at Northolt. Diagonally lower right on this 1915 map at 6ins to 1 mile is the MR's branch to
Acton, which is featured in the *St. Pancras to St. Albans album*. It was a freight-only route in 2006
and for long before that. Dog Lane was to become part of the North Circular Road.

27.    The eastern panorama from the North Circular Road in about 1937 has the LNER tracks
to the right of the telegraph poles and the depot lines curving lower left. To the left of the station
is the Met goods yard, which was open from 1st January 1894 to April 1958. On the right is the
ex-GCR coal yard; this was in use from 26th July 1898 until 4th March 1968. (Stations UK)

28.     The view towards London on 3rd October 1948 has the original tracks on the right, with the station building above them and the former MR bridge in the distance. The name was initially "Kingsbury & Neasden", but the words were reversed in 1910 and only "Neasden" was used after 1932. (G.Kerley/HLHC)

29.     The rear of the train is in the station in this 1983 view from the entrance to the depot. A subway to the island platform was provided for staff in 1922. Featured is the massive bridge for the dual carriageway of the North Circular Road. (J.C.Gillham)

30.    The original building was photographed in 1987, after the contrasting flat roof and glazed panels had been added. The central part of the structure had been rebuilt about 20 years earlier, when the main pitch was lost. (D.A.Thompson)

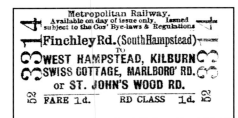

# NEASDEN DEPOT

XIV. A clear strip down the centre of this 1935 map marks the no-mans land between the former GCR tracks (left) and the Met's four running lines and its extensive 1888 works, carriage sidings, engine sheds and power station. The last two are top right, 'Chy.' marking the location of the chimneys. The dots top right are in the centre of the River Brent. The scale is about 17ins to 1 mile.

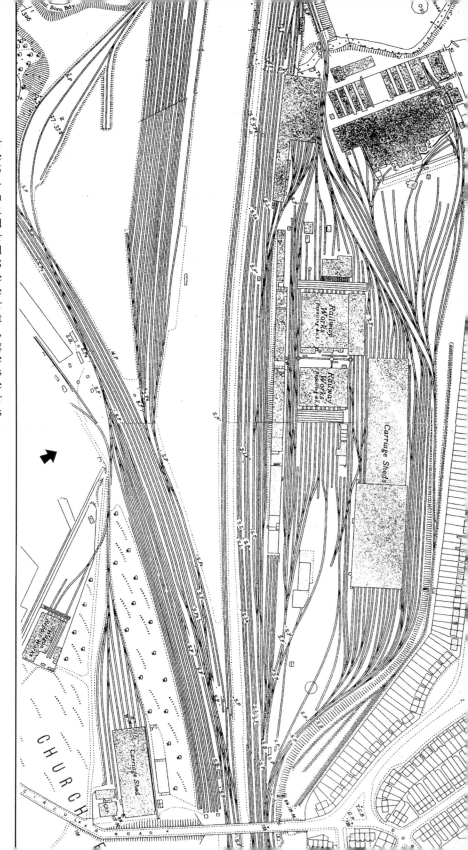

31.    A panorama from about 1915 has the carriage sheds on the right and the tall stores building on the left, as workers make their way home. The chimneys of the power station are in the background. The Met's first works was at Edgware Road. (G.Kerley coll./HLHC)

32.    A view from the GCR boundary on 24th June 1914 features Bo-Bo "Camel-Back" electric locomotive no. 1. It was one of ten obtained in 1905; they had Westinghouse electrical equipment in Metropolitan-Cammell bodies; these had sliding doors. (K.Nunn/LCGB)

33.     Part of the LT steam fleet was recorded in two photographs on 11th July 1936. On the left is class H 4-4-4T no. 103 and class G 0-6-4T no. 97 is on the right. In the background is another class H, no. 105. (H.C.Casserley)

34.     The elegance of the class H design is evident as K class 2-6-4T no. 116 takes water. These locos were amongst 18 taken over by the LNER to work trains north of Rickmansworth. LT retained 11 steam and 20 electric locomotives. (H.C.Casserley)

35.    The old iron engine shed was replaced by this structure in 1936. It was photographed in 1946 in the presence of class A 4-4-0T no. L45. Its large pipes were for condensing exhaust steam in the water tanks when working underground. (H.C.Casserley)

36.    A glimpse from a passing Marylebone train includes the remains of an 0-6-2T and much of the power station. Its chimneys were blown up on 28th September 1969. (D.B.Clayton)

37.    Recorded on 4th October 1958 were nos L50 (right) and L53 (in the shed). No. L45 is in the centre. (R.M.Casserley)

38.    No. 53 was a class B 0-6-0ST, built by Peckett in 1897. Steam was used longer by LT than BR, some ex-GWR locos being in use until 1971 for engineering trains. (H.Davies)

41.　　Seen in about 1925 are four platforms. Two were available to park event visitors from 1893, the station opening fully on 12th May 1894. Two more were added in January 1914, when quadruple track reached here. The electric/steam locomotive change took place here instead of Harrow-on-the-Hill sometimes, to reduce light engine running. (Stations UK)

42.　　A further two platforms were completed on 24th February 1932, for Stanmore trains, and a single line flyunder gave tube trains direct access to Neasden Depot from 27th March 1939. The Art Deco styling is evident in this 1981 view of platforms 5 and 6. (A.C.Mott)

43.　　The signal box is seen in September 2005; it originally had 59 levers, but the frame was replaced by a push-button panel on 28th September 1954. The famous stadium was erected on part of the exhibition site, but this was being replaced when this photograph was taken. The station was being extensively upgraded to increase its passenger throughput, the work being completed in May 2006, long before the new stadium. (V.Mitchell)

# NORTH OF WEMBLEY PARK

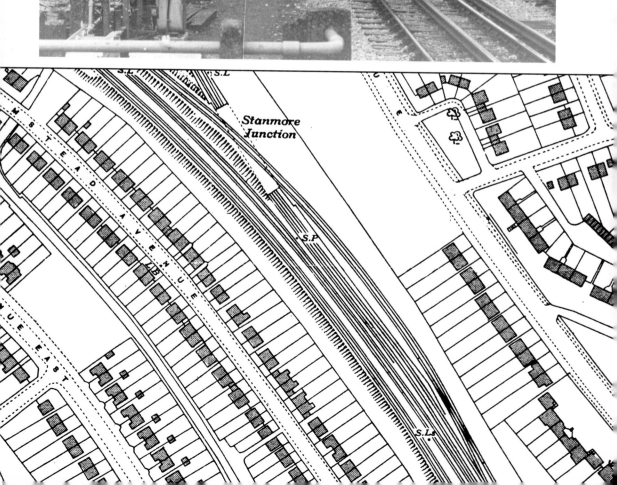

Stanmore
Junction

44. The nine roads shown in the carriage shed on the map were reduced to five. The 1932 structure was photographed in 1983 as a Jubilee Line train waits on the reversing siding to return to Charing Cross and a Baker Street train arrives on "Met Local"; "Met Fast" is on the right. (F.Hornby)

XVII. The 1940 edition shows the 1939 flyunder for Stanmore trains near the words "Stanmore Junction". This was no longer true, as it was further south by that time. Two additional tracks between it and the station came into use in June 1954.

45. A Met northbound stopping train is on the left on 18th August 2006, as another unit stands on one of the recently relaid sidings. The shed had been demolished in the previous Winter. (V.Mitchell)

# KINGSBURY

XVIII. The 1935 edition shows partial development of the area, which was totally rural when the four-mile long Stanmore branch opened on 10th December 1932.

46.    The station entrance (right) was made central to the commercial hub of the area, the post office being opposite. The transport of a local tradesman is included in this view from soon after the opening. (G.Kerley/HLHC)

47.    The ticket hall is in line with the fog repeater signal in this northward view from 29th November 1947. The first UK example of Central Train Control was to be found on the branch in 1932-39, it being based in the box at Wembley Park. (G.Kerley/HLHC)

# QUEENSBURY

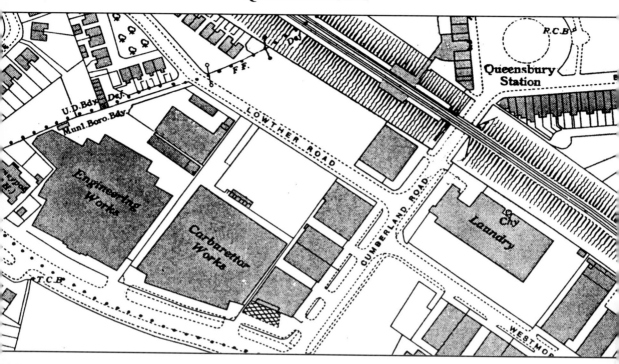

XIX.    Kingsbury was an old parish of 1828 acres, but Queensbury was the notion of an estate developer keen to imply status, despite the industrial areas. This extract is from 1940.

48.    A small wooden halt came into use on 16th December 1934 and traffic gradually developed as building work proceeded. Much of this was done on the site of Stag Lane Aerodrome, which explains the roads having many aviation names. Concrete platforms arrived in 1977, the year of the Queen's Jubilee - the trains were two years late. The photograph is from 1959. (Stations UK)

49.    The platform buildings date from 1950, but the entrance terrace was completed in 1936, the latter being photographed 70 years later, along with the bridge. (V.Mitchell)

METROPOLITAN RAILWAY.
Available on day of issue only.
issued subject to the Company's
By-laws, Regulations, Bills and Notices.
Stanmore
Stanmore                    Stanmore
TO
CANONS PARK, EDGWARE
Canons Park, Edgware    Canons Park, Edgware
2½d. FIRST CLASS 2½d.
10.DEC32
000

# CANONS PARK

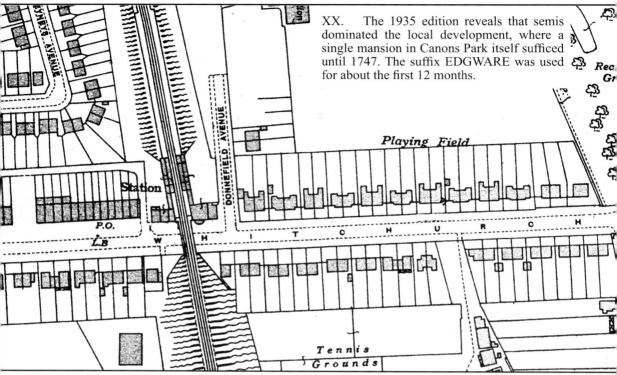

XX.  The 1935 edition reveals that semis dominated the local development, where a single mansion in Canons Park itself sufficed until 1747. The suffix EDGWARE was used for about the first 12 months.

50.  "The Railway World Special" was hauled by Met loco no. 1 *John Lyon* on 21st May 1955 and it is seen returning from Stanmore. It was one of 20 built in 1921-23, although two were partial rebuilds from the original batches. All carried names from 1927. (N.W.Sprinks)

51.     A 1959 view towards Stanmore features the early style of rivetted canopy. The platforms deteriorated to the point where the station was closed during August and September 1993 for their complete replacement. (Stations UK)

52.     Two entrances serve the ticket hall, which has pleasant skylights in a vaulted ceiling, wooden wall panels and tiled flooring. The toilets are equally impeccable. The smart exterior is seen in 2006. (V.Mitchell)

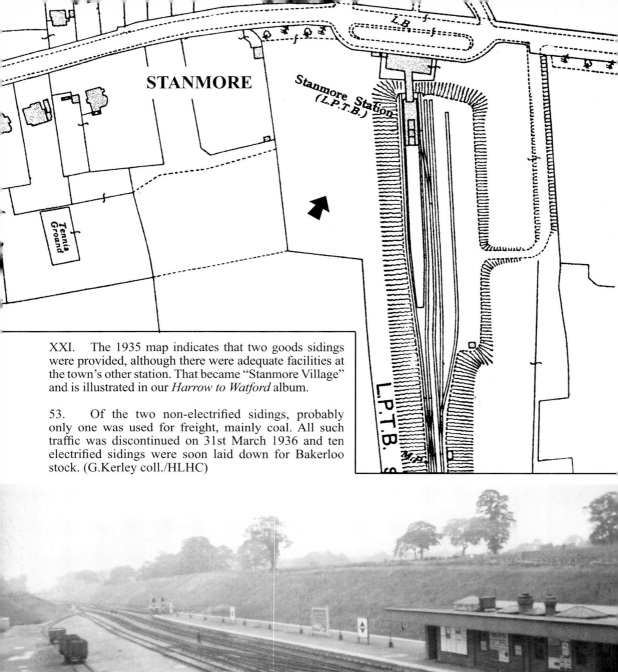

**STANMORE**

Stanmore Station (L.P.T.B.)

Tennis Ground

L.B.

L.P.T.B. S

XXI.   The 1935 map indicates that two goods sidings were provided, although there were adequate facilities at the town's other station. That became "Stanmore Village" and is illustrated in our *Harrow to Watford* album.

53.     Of the two non-electrified sidings, probably only one was used for freight, mainly coal. All such traffic was discontinued on 31st March 1936 and ten electrified sidings were soon laid down for Bakerloo stock. (G.Kerley coll./HLHC)

54.	There were many features in common with the Met's 1925 terminus at Watford. Seen soon after opening, the exterior was little changed in 2006. The notable improvement was the extension of the canopy for the benefit of bus passengers. (G.Kerley coll./HLHC)

55.	One of the Met's two single cars (no. 2769) sufficed for the off-peak traffic until November 1938. A two-car set was used subsequently, but a change at Wembley Park was still necessary. The roof of the platform staircase is evident on the left, on 5th August 1934. The rear-view mirror improved safety, a feature lacking on modern locos and one that could help bring derailed freight trains to a rapid stop. (K.Nunn/LCGB)

56.    The Southern Counties Touring Society ran a train on 1st October 1961 using 0-4-4T no. L44. It can be seen at the other end of its journey, near New Cross, in picture nos 46 and 50 in our *East London Line album*. It is preserved at the Buckinghamshire Railway Centre. (H.C.Casserley)

57.    Work was in progress on 11th August 2006 to prepare for the construction of an additional platform. This would increase line capacity at times of peak demand at Wembley Park. The 1939 signal box had stood on the right. Its 47-lever frame allowed 3½ minute headways. A new system in 1955 reduced the figure to 2. (V.Mitchell)

# PRESTON ROAD

58.     Initially, two short platforms were provided on the other side of the road bridge at the suggestion of Uxendon Shooting Club, which hosted the teams at the Olympic Games at White City in 1908. The request stop opened on 21st May of that year. This platform came into use in 1931-32 and is seen on 22nd October 1938. (G.Kerley/HLHC)

59.     The exterior was recorded on 1st June 1947. The walkways behind the shops and flats are evident in the previous photograph. The lack of traffic is a reminder that fuel rationing was still in force, as was food incidentally. (G.Kerley/HLHC)

# NORTHWICK PARK

60. Opened as "Northwick Park & Kenton" on 28th June 1923, the suffix was abandoned on 15th March 1937. The subway passes under all six tracks, as well as the island plaltform. (G.Kerley/HLHC)

61. The original halt was replaced by the structure seen, in about 1931. This northward view from 1955 includes the guard's starting signal wires and

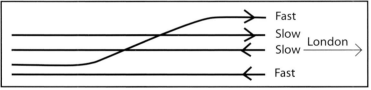

supporting brackets. The wide space between the two left electrified tracks was occupied (until 1948) by the up fast Met track. This crossed over to gain an eastern position by a doubly conflicting crossing situated between Northwick Park and Preston Road. This track then matched up with the revised track plan between there and Finchley Road. (Stations UK)

# HARROW-ON-THE-HILL

62.     Trains for the Aylesbury route changed locomotives here until 5th January 1925. "Camel-Backs" nos 1 and 9 stand with 0-4-4T no. 79 on 25th September 1915, near Station Road. (K.Nunn/LCGB)

63.     The main entrance was on the south side when photographed in about 1933. The 1914 map shows it facing fields. This was (and is) the first station from London to have platforms for GCR line trains. It was a terminus in 1880-85, after which trains ran to Pinner. (G.Kerley coll./HLHC)

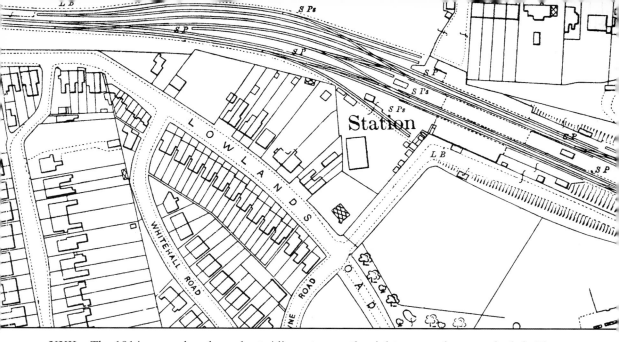

XXII. The 1914 survey has three short sidings, two on the right page and one on the left. There are also carriage sidings on the left; the goods yard was further west and is shown on the next two maps. The suffix was added on 1st June 1894.

64.     There were four platforms from 21st June 1908 and six from 1939. Although the six platform faces were made by late 1939 by turning the outer platforms into islands, the new platforms remained trackless until 1948. The 1925 track plan shown in map XXI in *Marylebone to Rickmansworth* remained in use until 1948, hence the need for the conflicting crossing between Northwick Park and Preston Road. This view west is from 27th February 1938 and has the carriage sidings in the distance. There was a short siding to the left of the water tower, which served a bay platform for three-coach Uxbridge trains in the early years of the branch. (G.Kerley/HLHC)

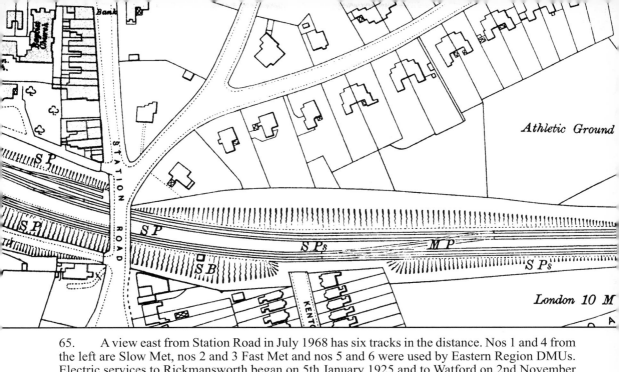

65.     A view east from Station Road in July 1968 has six tracks in the distance. Nos 1 and 4 from the left are Slow Met, nos 2 and 3 Fast Met and nos 5 and 6 were used by Eastern Region DMUs. Electric services to Rickmansworth began on 5th January 1925 and to Watford on 2nd November of that year. (J.C.Gillham)

66. An unusual railtour operated on 16th July 1972, using two former Met locomotives. They all had two types of coupling and dual braking systems. No. 5 was named *John Hampden:* it can be found in London's Transport Museum collection.
(D.Trevor Rowe)

67. A 1982 panorama includes the entire station, the ticket hall being above the centre platforms. The 1908 subway still linked the platforms and the former goods lifts were eventually made available for passengers.
(D.A.Thompson)

68. The north side was redeveloped around 1980 and a new entrance was provided close to the bus station, visible through the arch. Another bus station was created on the other side of the station, one of the busiest on LT. The southern part was extended upwards in the later 1980s.
(V.Mitchell)

73.     The station opened on 17th November 1913 following local pressure and basic timber-framed buildings were provided. Much lengthened, they were photographed in 1972 and reconstructed in 1991 to a similar outline. (Stations UK)

74.     Light and airy, the 1991 ticket office was pictured in August 2006. The area is wooded and peaceful in contrast to Harrow-on-the-Hill. (V.Mitchell)

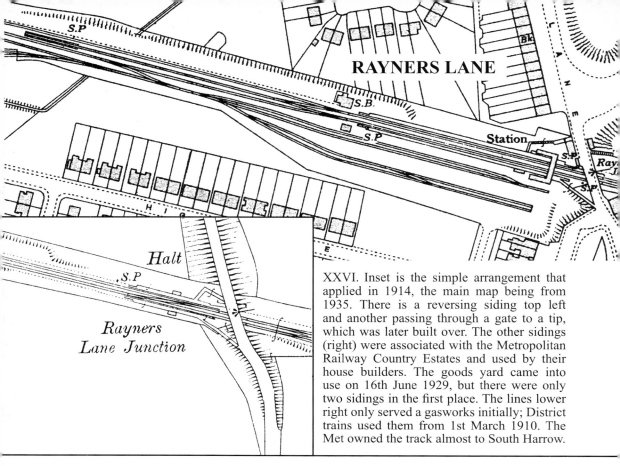

**RAYNERS LANE**

*Halt*

*S.P*

*Rayners Lane Junction*

XXVI. Inset is the simple arrangement that applied in 1914, the main map being from 1935. There is a reversing siding top left and another passing through a gate to a tip, which was later built over. The other sidings (right) were associated with the Metropolitan Railway Country Estates and used by their house builders. The goods yard came into use on 16th June 1929, but there were only two sidings in the first place. The lines lower right only served a gasworks initially; District trains used them from 1st March 1910. The Met owned the track almost to South Harrow.

75.     Contractors' wagons stand on the running lines shortly before the junction was completed in 1904; the sawmill is in the right background. Daniel Rayner's name lives on; he was a late Victorian farmer in the area. (F.Moores/HLHC)

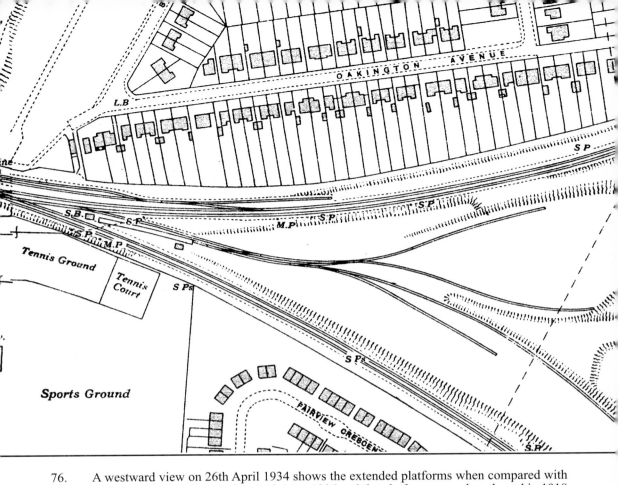

76.    A westward view on 26th April 1934 shows the extended platforms when compared with the inset plan. The halt had opened on 26th May 1906 and the platforms were lengthened in 1918 and 1927. Roundel and diamond signs coexist, unusually. (G.Kerley/HLHC)

77.    The roadside ticket office lasted until the present spacious building was opened on 8th August 1938. The bridge parapet is on the left. In 1930, there were 22,000 passengers; this increased to 4 million in 1937. (G.Kerley/HLHC)

78.    It is 7th March 1936 and a rare record of a Met freight train was made from the rural road bridge. No. 91 was an 0-6-2T. (P.Q.Treloar coll.)

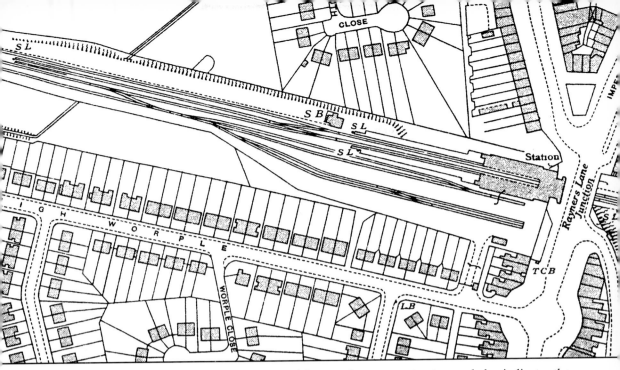

XXVII. The 1939 edition gives the outline of the prominent new structure and also indicates the increase in width of the bridge.

79.    The goods yard closed on 10th August 1964 and two of the sidings had been lifted by the time the photographer had arrived on 8th November 1965. (J.C.Gillham)

80.    A further view, but from 5th June 1968, shows that two were retained. The remainder of the yard was fenced off as a car park. Piccadilly Line trains began using the station on 23rd October 1933; one is about to reverse. (J.C.Gillham)

81.    An Uxbridge to Aldgate via Harrow service arrives on 26th April 2006. District Line trains first appeared here on 1st March 1910. The Met had promoted "Harrow Garden Village" in the 1930s, but the name did not last. Initially 1600 houses were built on 214 acres. (M.Turvey)

82.    The extension of the station beyond the adjacent building lines makes a bold statement of the importance of the railway historically, developmentally and commercially. (V.Mitchell)

# EASTCOTE

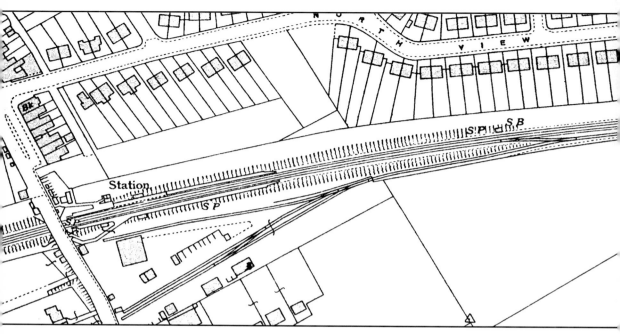

XXVIII. The 1935 edition has inclined paths down to the platforms from the road. There was no goods yard on the 1914 map. The one shown closed on 10th August 1964.

83.    A southward view from 1938 includes the simple building (left) in its original form and shortly before demolition. (Lens of Sutton)

84.    A mixture of buildings was found by the photographer on a wet day in April 1934. In the right background is a Met electrical sub-station. (G.Kerley/HLHC)

85.    Curves and straight lines were used to good effect in the rebuilding in 1939, as at Rayners Lane but at different angles. The photograph is from 11th August 2006. (V.Mitchell)

86.    On the same day, Piccadilly and Metropolitan trains pass. Modern PA and lighting sit comfortably with the earlier styles. (V.Mitchell)

# RUISLIP MANOR

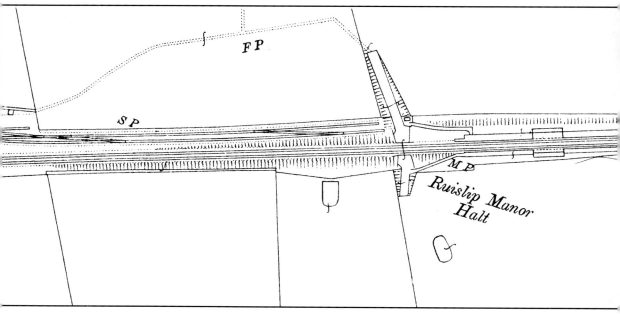

XXIX. The 1914 survey has the curious phenomena of a bridge, but no road, and a footpath which leads to the next station.

87.    This southward view from 1932 includes the hut and two paths shown on the map. The halt opened on 5th August 1912, but closed for two years at the end of World War I. Passengers' muddy boots would be stored in the booking office during their working day. (G.Kerley/HLHC)

88. Annual passenger figures rose from 17,000 in 1931 to 1,262,500 in 1937, when this photograph was taken. New buildings are taking shape in the background. (Stations UK)

89. Both platforms were rebuilt in sequence in 2005; this is the view from the up one on 28th September of that year. Fresh shelters were added behind the camera. (V.Mitchell)

90. Seen on the same day, the entire exterior was subject to renovation. The end result in 2006 was startling and sparkling. (V.Mitchell)

# RUISLIP

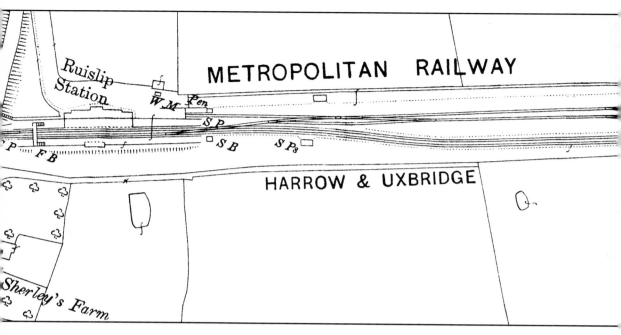

XXX. The 1914 edition contains part of the sidings, their eastern ends being included on the previous map. W.M. indicates Weighing Machine.

91.     The station is seen nearing completion in the Autumn of 1903, but a siding was still in place on the site of the approach road. This was the only intermediate station on the branch to have a permanent building for many years. The footbridge was moved nearer to it in 1928. Oil lighting was used until 1905. (G.Kerley coll./HLHC)

92.    The opening train on 4th July 1904 was hauled by 0-4-4T no. 1. Electric traction began on 1st January 1905. The 0-4-4T was later renumbered L44 and appears elsewhere in this volume; it was built at Neasden in 1898. (P.Q.Treloar coll.)

93.    This panorama is from 26th April 1934, when the transition from diamonds to roundels was taking place. This view has changed little in over 70 years, as have the next two. (G.Kerley/HLHC)

94. The date is 28th June 1947 and a Standard STL bus of LT waits, devoid of a route number. It is probably on an "emergency" service. (G.Kerley/HLHC)

95. The roof was added to the footbridge soon after it was moved in 1928. Car 10023 leads a Piccadilly Line train of 1938 stock, bound for Uxbridge on 26th October 1963. (J.C.Gillham)

96.    The same train is departing east later that day, carrying the then obligatory oil lamp. The coal yard siding was in use until 10th August 1964. The area of the sidings was subsequently devoted to car parking. (J.C.Gillham)

97.    The photographer moved back to include the signal box, which was still standing in 2006, complete with lever frame. Note that one siding was electrified and that terminating trains could start from the down platform. (J.C.Gillham)

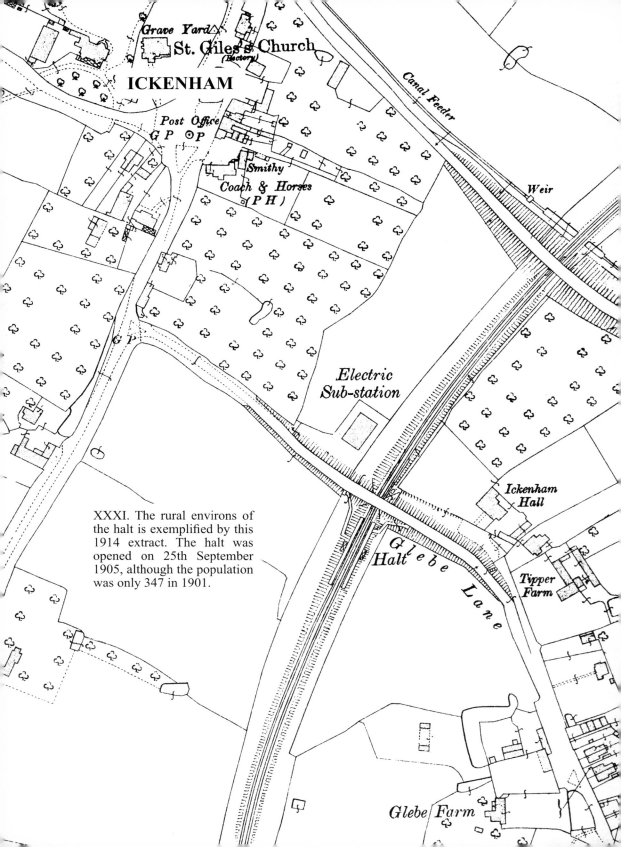

Grave Yard △

St. Giles's Church
(Rectory)

**ICKENHAM**

Canal Feeder

Post Office
G P ⊙ P

Smithy

Coach & Horses
( P H )

Weir

G P

Electric
Sub-station

Ickenham
Hall

XXXI. The rural environs of
the halt is exemplified by this
1914 extract. The halt was
opened on 25th September
1905, although the population
was only 347 in 1901.

*Glebe Lane*

Halt Lane

Tipper
Farm

*Glebe Farm*

98.     Initially, the platforms would accommodate only 3-car trains of the type illustrated soon after opening. Lengthening of the platforms took place in 1922. (G.Kerley coll./HLHC)

99.     Improvements followed in the form of a "Tudor" ticket office in 1910; it was photographed in March 1934. Its position is made clear in the next picture. (G.Kerley coll./HLHC)

100. Solid platforms eventually arrived; they are seen in 1934. On the skyline is the gable end of the sub-station, which served the west end of the branch. A connection to Ruislip Depot was laid from the down line, east of the station. (G.Kerley coll./HLHC)

101. Most of the buildings were reconstructed around 1971 and are seen in this and the next photograph in August 2006. Digital displays and CCTV complete the modern scene. (V.Mitchell)

102. The entrance was somewhat restricted during youthful acrobatic performances, but motorists have the benefit of a direct staircase down to the car park. A generous waiting room arrived on the westbound platform in 1993. (V.Mitchell)

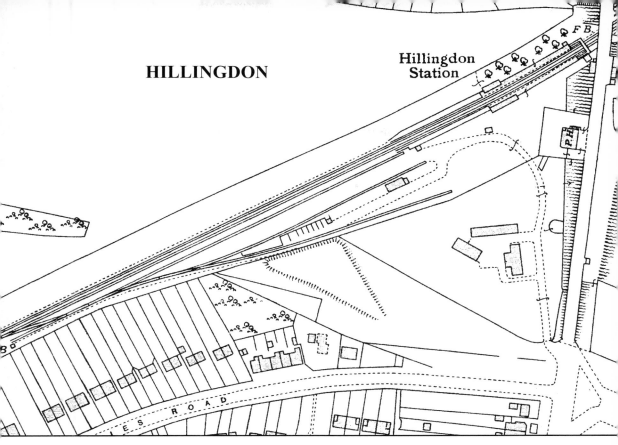

# HILLINGDON

Hillingdon
Station

XXXII.  The station opened later than the others, on 10th December 1923. It is shown on the 1934 edition. The goods yard was in use until 10th August 1964.

103.	The entrance was at the south end of the footbridge and was photographed in 1934. The suffix (Swakeleys) was added at that time and was in intermittent use subsequently. (G.Kerley coll./HLHC)

104.    Lengthy platform canopies had appeared by the time that this photograph was taken in 1959. The original ticket office is in the background. (Stations UK)

105.    A 1963 picture features 1938 Piccadilly stock destined for the far end of the line at Cockfosters. Everything within sight was demolished in September 1992 to allow realignment of the A40. (J.C.Gillham)

106.     The work was undertaken between January 1991 and Autumn 1993 and the new dual carriageway passed under the railway where the old local road had gone over it. A Met train runs towards Uxbridge on 27th February 1996 and passes under the long footbridge from, appropriately, Long Lane. (F.Hornby)

107.     Modernistic train sheds at different levels give excellent daylight distribution to the platforms, each of which is served by a lift. The ticket office is over the middle of this Met train and the new bridge for Long Lane is behind it. (M.Turvey)

# UXBRIDGE

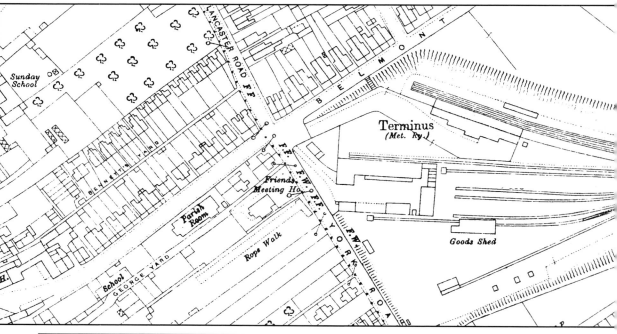

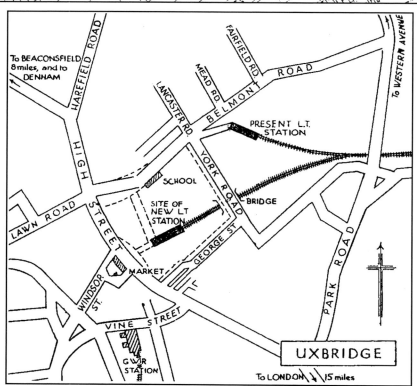

XXXIII. The 1914 edition has the passenger terminus near Belmont Road, a suffix used by Bradshaw, but not the Met or LT. The two longest goods sidings served warehouses and were later shortened. By 1934 a crane had been erected in the yard, which closed on 1st May 1939.

XXXIV. A 1937 plan shows that the alignment of the route to the new terminus was to be on that of the southernmost siding. It would reach the town centre at the High Street.

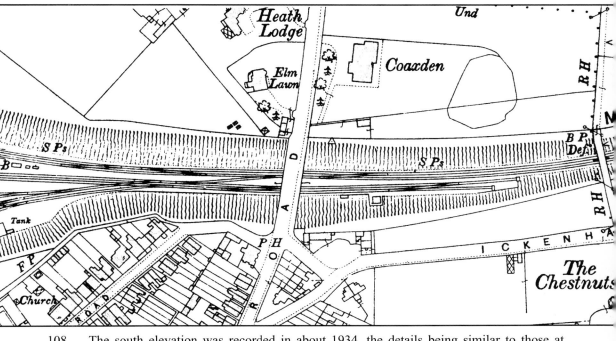

108.    The south elevation was recorded in about 1934, the details being similar to those at
Ruislip. The population was a little over 3000 in 1901 and almost 65,000 in 1961.
(G.Kerley/HLHC)

109.    Met trains used the platform on the left, but when District trains were eventually allowed in on 1st March 1910, passengers had to use the one with no shelter and walk round the buffers in the distance. (G.Kerley/HLHC)

→
110.    A Met train of T stock was recorded in 1937. Prior to this LT designation, it was known as MW stock; the W indicated Westinghouse air brakes. The MV units were similar, but were fitted with vacuum brakes and buffers. The front panel beading was later removed from some cars; see picture 4 for the overpainted version. (G.Kerley/HLHC)

→
111.    The new terminus is seen under construction; it was ready for the opening on 4th December 1938. Two-foot gauge track is on both platforms in this view from early 1937. A mammoth tusk was discovered, but left undisturbed. (Stations UK)

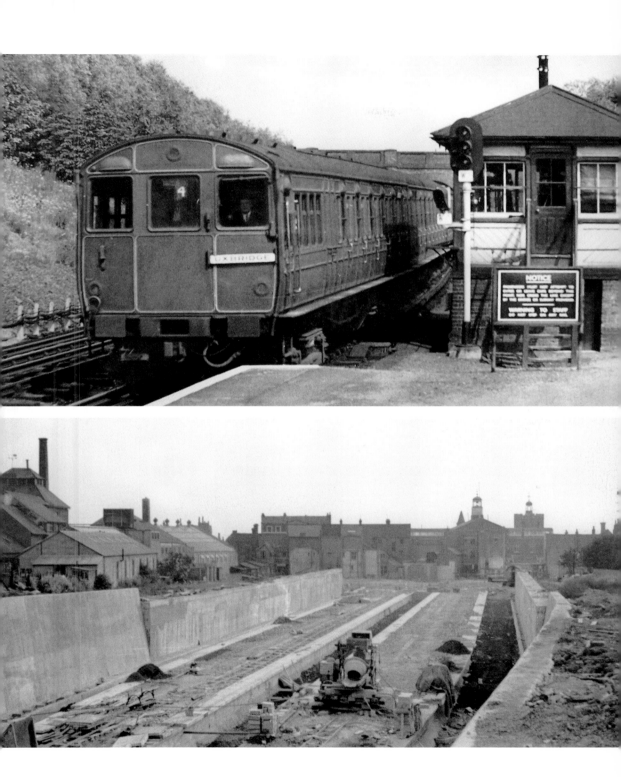

112.    A special train (left) ran on 4th July 1954
(the Golden Jubilee of the line) and its openable
windows gave the opportunity to record some of
the eleven carriage sidings, during the descent to     113.    The relative high level of the carriage
the station, under Park Road. The loco is 0-4-4T       sidings is evident as no. 16 *Oliver Goldsmith*
no. L44, which hauled the opening train.               returns the stock of the special train to the station
(H.C.Casserley)                                        on 4th July 1954. (D.Trevor Rowe)

114.    Trolleybuses terminated in the forecourt from 3rd March 1954, but only for a few weeks
while road repairs took place in the High Street. However, the wires remained in place for more
than six years. (J.C.Gillham)

115.  The goods shed and the original passenger station were both extended northwards to provide further accommodation for Alfred Button & Sons, grocery wholesalers. The view is from September 1960. (J.C.Gillham)

116.  The fine symmetry of the vaulted roof on its multitude of concrete buttresses and the excellent provision of natural lighting are evident in this 1988 study. After 88 minutes, one could visit the similar northern terminal of the Piccadilly Line. (A.C.Mott)

117.  The pedestrian approach has continuity of style with the train shed, giving the impression of seamless travel. The station was unusual amongst those of LT in having a licensed restaurant. The steps (left) are close to it and lead to the north entrance. (A.C.Mott)

118.    The embracing curves of the west facade draw the potential passenger to the fluted columns at the end of the well-lit and lengthy hallway, just seen. (F.Hornby)

119.    A gleaming 1938 unit took centre stage (or the centre road) on 4th July 2004 for the celebrations of 100 years of the route, an event worth straining the trouser seams for. (Dr. J.S.Manners)

120.    The north entrance is an insignificant affair, right of centre. However, its importance is that it gives access to a large number of bus stops from where it is easy to travel to much of outer West London and also Brunel University. (V.Mitchell)

**Uxbridge Vine Street station can be seen in pictures
105 to 120 in *Ealing to Slough* and
Uxbridge High Street appears in nos 60 to 65 in our
*Paddington to Princes Risborough* album.
*Shepherds Bush and Uxbridge Tramways*
illustrates the light railway to the town, in use until 1936.**

# ON WHIT-SUNDAY, 11th MAY,

## (ALSO EVERY SUNDAY),

## and ‡WHIT-MONDAY,‡

# CHEAP TICKETS

WILL BE ISSUED

## From LONDON Stations TO

## ‡HARROW‡, RAYNERS LANE,

# EASTCOTE,

# RUISLIP MANOR, RUISLIP,

# ICKENHAM & UXBRIDGE.

AS UNDER:—

| FROM | RETURN FARES, THIRD CLASS. | | | | | |
|---|---|---|---|---|---|---|
| | To ‡ Harrow. ‡ | To Rayners Lane Halt. | To Eastcote. | To Ruislip Manor, Ruislip, & Ickenham. | To Uxbridge. | |
| NEW CROSS (L.B.& S.C.) | — | 1/4 | 1/5 | 1/6 | 1/9 | Available for Return by any Train on day of issue only. |
| Surrey Docks | — | 1/3 | 1/4 | 1/5 | 1/7 | |
| Rotherhithe ... | | | | | | |
| Wapping ... | — | 1/2 | 1/3 | 1/4 | 1/6 | |
| Shadwell ... | | | | | | |
| St. Mary's (Whitechapel)... | 11d. | 1/1 | 1/2 | 1/3 | 1/5 | |
| Aldgate East ... | | | | | | |
| Cannon Street ... | | | | | | |
| Monument ... | | | | | | |
| Mark Lane ... | 11d. | 1/1 | 1/1 | 1/3 | 1 5 | |
| Aldgate ... | | | | | | |
| Liverpool Street ... | | | | | | |
| Moorgate Street ... | | | | | | |
| Aldersgate ... | 11d. | 1/1 | 1/1 | 1/2 | 1/5 | |
| Farringdon Street ... | 11d. | 1/1 | 1/1 | 1/2 | 1/4 | |
| King's Cross ... | | | | | | |
| Euston Square ... | 10d. | 1/- | 1/- | 1/1 / 1/- | 1/3 | |
| Portland Road ... | | | | | | |
| BAKER STREET ... | 10d. | 11d. | 11d. | 11d. | 1/3 | |
| St. John's Wood Road ... | | | | | | |
| Marlboro' Road ... | | | | | | |
| Swiss Cottage ... | 9d. | 11d. | 11d. | 11d. | 1/2 | |
| Finchley Road ... | | | | | | |
| West Hampstead ... | 9d. | 10d. | 11d. | 11d. | 1/2 | |
| Kilburn–Brondesbury | No Bookings | 10d. | 11d. | 11d. | 1/2 | |
| Willesden Green ... | | 10d. | 10d. | 10d. | 1/2 | |
| Edgware Road ... | 10d. | 11d. | 11d. | 11d. | 1/3 | |
| Paddington Praed Street... | 11d. | 11d. | 11d. | 11d. | 1/3 | |
| „ „ Bishop's Road | | | | | | |
| Bayswater ... | | | | | | |
| Notting Hill Gate ... | | | | | | |
| High Street, Kensington ... | 11d. | 11d. | 1/- | 1/1 | 1/3 | |
| Gloucester Road ... | | | | | | |
| South Kensington ... | | | | | | |

## TICKETS WILL BE ISSUED AS UNDER:—

TO HARROW (on SUNDAYS only) by all Trains from Baker Street between 2.0 and 3.48 p.m., viz.— 2.10, 2.35, 2.43, 3.0, 3.1, 3.22, 3.30, 3.48 p.m.

To Rayners Lane Halt
  Eastcote Halt
  Ruislip Manor Halt — By all Trains from Baker Street up to 5.44 p.m. on
  Ruislip            Sundays, and up to 5.41 p.m. on Whit-Monday.
  Ickenham Halt
  Uxbridge

‡ No Bookings to Harrow on Whit-Monday.

## Through Tickets at Cheap Fares will also be issued from Stations on the Bakerloo Line to all stations except Harrow.

Here we see the opportunities for Londoners to use Met trains for a day in the country in 1913.

Such opportunities existed in many parts of Metro-land in the 1920s, these dwellings being near the top of the range.

# HIGHFIELDS ESTATE, HILLINGDON

SECTION OF ESTATE SHOWING ARTISTIC ARRANGEMENT OF HOUSES

# *Something Different!*

DISCRIMINATING House-Seekers will find their ideal on the Highfields Estate, Hillingdon —a model Tudor village of charming houses artistically grouped in the form of fascinating courts. Well built, skilfully planned residences available from £995 freehold—free of all road charges. Exceptionally easy deferred purchase terms. Best quality materials only used. Each individual house designed by and built under strict supervision of qualified architects. Excellent gardens; exceptional train service; splendid shopping and educational facilities. Inspect them this week-end—you will not be pressed to buy. Cheap fares from all Metro. Stns. Estate within 5 mins. walk of Hillingdon Stn.

## TUDOR HOUSING COMPANY
## HIGHFIELDS ESTATE, HILLINGDON
### Telephone: PINNER 634

# MP Middleton Press

**Easebourne Lane, Midhurst, West Sussex.**
**GU29 9AZ  Tel:01730 813169**

EVOLVING THE ULTIMATE RAIL ENCYCLOPEDIA

www.middletonpress.co.uk  email:info@middletonpress.co.uk

A-0 906520  B-1 873793  C-1 901706  D-1 904474

OOP Out of print at time of printing - Please check availability  BROCHURE AVAILABLE SHOWING NEW TITLES